YOUR KNOWLEDGE HAS

Bibliographic information published by the German National Library:

The German National Library lists this publication in the National Bibliography; detailed bibliographic data are available on the Internet at http://dnb.dnb.de .

Imprint:

Copyright © 2016 GRIN Verlag, Open Publishing GmbH
Print and binding: Books on Demand GmbH, Norderstedt Germany
ISBN: 9783668262508

This book at GRIN:

http://www.grin.com/en/e-book/322697/skype-or-slack-swot-analysis-of-online-communication-tools

Pirooz Pejman

Skype or Slack? SWOT analysis of online communication tools

GRIN Publishing

GRIN - Your knowledge has value

Since its foundation in 1998, GRIN has specialized in publishing academic texts by students, college teachers and other academics as e-book and printed book. The website www.grin.com is an ideal platform for presenting term papers, final papers, scientific essays, dissertations and specialist books.

Visit us on the internet:

http://www.grin.com/

http://www.facebook.com/grincom

http://www.twitter.com/grin_com

Online communication tools - SWOT analysis - Instant messaging tools - Skype and Slack

May 2016

Written by *Captain Creative*

(Pirooz Pejman)

Cologne, Germany

www.tedtranslation.com

Table of contents

1   Introduction

In today's world, the possibilities for communication via Internet have become very common both in private and business matters. Messages can be sent from one corner of the world to the other in the blink of an eye, be it via e-mail, as the technological advanced version of letters, instant messaging with the frequent extra opportunity of a video talk and Internet telephony (VoIP) as a much more inexpensive way of phoning via Internet. In a rapidly increasing globalized world now more than ever, time is money when it comes to entrepreneurial actions and at the same time of essence for private purposes as we have got used to rapid communication. As an inevitable consequence, people's attention span as well as patience related to communication or demanding access to information has been reducing drastically. Expectations regarding a safe and extremely fast way of communicating are very high and continue to rise.

In the present paper, various ways of virtual communication will be illustrated. In this connection, first common possibilities of communicating virtually such as e-mail, instant messaging and VoIP will be presented before two major and popular instant messaging tools available on the Internet, Slack and Skype, are going to be examined in greater detail by pointing out their strength, weaknesses, opportunities and threats with the help of a SWOT-analysis. This is supposed to figure out the most effective, efficient, useful and safe communication instant messaging tool. Further, it aims at figuring out which tool(s) will prevail in the future and therefore stand(s) the test of time.

A conclusion will summarize the findings.

2   Common online communication tools

2.1   E-mail

2.1.1 General Information

The e-mail (electronic mail) represents the first and original communication tool of the Internet and has taken the place of postal mails for some time now. The reason for this relies undoubtedly on the fact that e-mails can transfer information in the form of text or to a degree as files to any person around the world in seconds as long as the recipient possesses an e-mail account as well as an access to the Internet in any way. Not only can any message be composed much quicklier than a written letter, it can also be saved in a proper order on the online server of the respective provider. This way, one is able to find even very outdated messages that one might need for a particular purpose. Apart from that e-mails play an essential role concerning confirmation mails since online orders have become very common throughout all kind of customers worldwide. Moreover, e-mail has been enabling a way of communication between teachers or various instructors to keep in touch with the students' parents. Simultaneously, e-mails give students the chance to reach out to their teachers or instructors, respectively, when exams are just around the corner or presentations need to be held but urgent questions on the part of students have not been answered yet.[1]

2.1.2 SWOT-Analysis

In the following, a SWOT-Analysis is going to be carried out concerning "e-mails" as an online communication tool.

Strengths: An e-mail presents a convenient way of sending messages almost in real-time. Further information in forms of text files or pictures can be attached without any effort. This virtual communication tool is also a relevant part of online trading since it informs the customer of finalized orders right away. Also, in connection to applications, numerous enterprises require online applications that can only be realized by means of using an e-mail.

Weaknesses: For the e-mail is stored on the private inbox of the receiver on an online server, the recipient first must check his inbox to notice the new message unless a downloaded application on his or her smartphone informs him of any incoming e-mail. This leads directly to another deficit, the waiting period for a response on the part of a recipient. The amount of attachable files is sometimes limited subject to the respective inbox provider.

Opportunities: The main advantageous possibility is certainly to be found in the rapidness and convenience of applying e-mails as an online tool to communicate messages and information in general.

---

[1] Cf. Wikispaces: The Internet as a Communication tool. URL:
https://techforinstructionandassessment.wikispaces.com/The+Internet+as+a+Communication+Tool
retrieved: 03/06/16.

Threats: Errors concerning the online server where the inbox is stored on can hinder the accessibility to the file even if this happens very rarely. In case of a missing alerting system, the recipient can miss necessary and important messages or information which is due in particular circumstances.

2.2 Instant messaging tools

2.2.1 General Information

In the year 2004, instant messaging, usually abbreviated by IM, was used by more than 50 million US-Americans and had already been used more than e-mail by almost a quarter of them at that time. Compared to face-to-face communication, instant messaging comes second by a third of the people. If one takes a look at the various versions of messengers, one can always find the same structure. They usually consist of a buddy list, which contains friends, family members or other acquaintances one prefers to stay in contact with via IM.[2]

2.2.2 SWOT-Analysis

Strengths: A clear advantage is the immediate messaging at any time and the higher degree of convenience than e-mail since one does not have to log into one's account but can leave the respective messenger active all the time. The obvious difference between the two ways of linguistic exchange is that instant messaging takes place non-verbal. Moreover, it is both available for different smartphone systems such as Android in the version of for example Whatsapp or for computer based operating systems such as Windows like messengers of various providers. Further, common, daily emotional expressions, which are always presenting an aspect of someone's personality in a way, can be conveyed with the help of so-called "emoticons", downloadable in various types, often for free. It is not uncommon these days, especially between young people, to mix a variety of emoticons to express one's feelings. Further extras that messengers provide are letting your contacts know about your availability, your present location and even about your current emotional state depending on the individual messenger.[3] Moreover, a buddy list makes it possible for individuals to create their own list of

---

[2] Cf. Davey, T. et al. (2004): Instant messaging. Functions of a new communication tool. Indiana: University of Notre Dame, Department of Anthropology, Blum, S.(publ.), pp. 1 et seqq.
[3] Cf. ibid.

contacts and therefore provide so-called presence awareness, which means two users of each contact list always know about each other's current status.[4]

Weaknesses: A striking deficit of instant messaging is the lack of face-to-face interaction in order to convey emotions. There might be individually more complicated situations, in which an emoticon might not suffice to convey one's mixed messages.[5]

Opportunities: Personal relationships of short or long distance can both benefit from instant messaging as it helps the relationship to sustain a permanent communicative exchange. Because no face-to-face interaction is required, individuals can avoid a real confrontation with their dialogue partner by letting forward his or her message when he or she thinks of it and by not being forced to call or meet the person. This also facilitates conflict management and diminishes anxiety, in particular in relationships, regardless their private or professional nature.[6] However the different emoticons might look like in shape or color, they always put across an emotional message that at least to an extent might be considered as a surrogate for facial expressions and gestures.[7] Concerning the buddy list of a messenger, the individual has the option to divide individual contacts into particular groups in order to create specific social circles or identify them according to one's own will, respectively. This reminds of social separations that people consciously or unconsciously do anyway as everybody has his or her priorities. As a result, instant messaging simplifies this process in technological ways as mentioned above. Because individuals have complete control of the features of their messenger, they can decide themselves what they want to disclose besides having the option to block contacts that are disturbing to them or they do not want to have any "virtual" relation to anymore.[8]

Threats: Owing to the comfort that instant messaging provides when it comes to interpersonal communication, it could contribute to ignoring more and more face-to-face interaction that is essential for a healthy and functional human relationship.

---

[4] Cf. Alexander, P. (Entrepreneur, publ.): Should your business use instant messaging? URL: http://www.entrepreneur.com/article/81050 retrieved 03/10/16.
[5] Cf. Cf. Davey, T. et al. (2004): Instant messaging. Functions of a new communication tool. Indiana: University of Notre Dame, Department of Anthropology, Blum, S.(publ.), pp. 1 et seqq.
[6] Cf. Hertlein, K. M.; Ancheta, K.: Advantages and Disadvantages of Technology in Relationships: Findings from an Open-Ended Survey. In: The Qualitative Report 2014, vol. 19, article 22, p.5.
[7] Cf. To, N. M. L. (2008): Influence of emoticons on message interpretation in computer mediated communication. Academia (publ.), p.2.
[8] Cf. Davey, T. et al. (2004): Instant messaging. Functions of a new communication tool. Indiana: University of Notre Dame, Department of Anthropology, Blum, S.(publ.), pp. 1 et seqq.

Further, emotionally more complex situations between two dialogue partners that are communicated with the help of instant messaging can result in misunderstanding and therefore do not correspond the initial intention of the sender or receiver of the expression, respectively. Another critical aspect is that instant messaging inevitably results in a constant disclosure of information related to one's privacy.[9]

2.3   VoIP - Internet telephony

2.3.1 General Information

VoIP, standing for Voice over Internet Protocol, is a way of online communication enabling a user to carry out voice calls by means of a broadband Internet connection. Depending on the individual service provider, phone calls can be made only to subscribers of the same provider or even unlimitedly to anyone in possession of a telephone. Concerning the technical hardware the user needs a PC or Notebook with an Internet connection, being a cable modem or high speed connection such as DSL or a local area network. Some service providers offer the possibility to apply one's own key-operated telephone. In case of using a computer, a particular software as well as any type of microphone or headset is needed. For applying a key-operated telephone a VoIP adapter is required.[10]

2.3.2 SWOT-Analysis

Strengths: The virtual way of communicating via VoIP offers various strengths. First of all, a broadband Internet connection such as DSL or cable modem is sufficient to benefit from making a phone call via VoIP. Further, the user does not have to pay for the VoIP services as they are for free if the phone call is made from a computer to another. From a more fiscal perspective, Internet telephony exhibits a relatively low taxation compared to ordinarily local telephony. Further, VoIP phone calls can be carried out at any place as long as a broadband Internet connection is available which is pretty common in almost any household these days. Further, video conversations

---

[9] Cf. Hertlein, K. M.; Ancheta, K.: Advantages and Disadvantages of Technology in Relationships: Findings from an Open-Ended Survey. In: The Qualitative Report 2014, vol. 19, article 22, pp. 7 et seq.
[10] Cf. Federal Communications Commission: Voice Over Internet Protocol (VoIP). URL: https://www.fcc.gov/general/voice-over-internet-protocol-voip retrieved 3/10/16.

and conferences as well as audio conferences can be held via the Internet, pictures or any other files can be exchanged parallel to the conversation. In addition, VoIP offers a range of extra features such as call waiting, call forwarding, caller ID, voicemail or three-way calling.[11]

Weaknesses: An essential weakness of VoIP telephony is certainly the often poor quality of voice, which results in regular echo or static noises.[12] A further blind spot is the entire dependency on the individual broadband Internet connection, which significantly determines the voice quality of the VoIP call. Because VoIP works via the broadband Internet connection, it does not possess an internal power line the way a usual telephone line does. In addition, emergency phone calls cannot be carried out effectively since they cannot be traced back by operators.[13]

Opportunities: Due to low costs, the distance of the VoIP call does not matter. This way for example business affiliates can keep a steady communication involving low costs. In particular smaller business benefit as well as the international business trade profits from that. At the same time long-distance relationships which are becoming more and more usual due to globalization can be facilitated by enabling the partners to communicate more often. Lower expenses also result from the fact that no additional cables are necessary, which especially businesses benefit from for example in case of moving. As VoIP also comes along with manifold advanced communication features, it enables you to talk with two people simultaneously on the phone.[14] As a consequence, business or private matters can be taken care of more effectively and efficiently.[15]

Threats: Due to the lack of an integrated power line or battery, VoIP phone services will be useless in case of blackouts. Another particular disadvantage strikes the eye if it comes to an emergency call, which can decide on somebody's fate. In contrast to IP calls, VoIP phone calls are not able to be traced back by the phone companies

---

[11] Cf. TechandSeo: Advantages and Disadvantages of VoIP. URL: http://www.techandseo.com/2015/11/advantages-and-disadvantages-of-voip-voice-over-Internet-protocol retrieved 3/10/16.
[12] Cf. Kumar, A.: An overview of voice over Internet Protocol (VoIP). In: Rivier College Online Academic Journal, vol. 2, no. 1, spring 2006, p. 9.
[13] Cf. DeSantis, M. (2008): Understanding Voice over Internet Protocol. US-CERT (publ.) URL: https://www.us-cert.gov/sites/default/files/publications/understanding_voip.pdf p.3., retrieved 3/10/16.
[14] Cf. verizon wireless: Support. 3-Way Calling FAQs. URL: http://www.verizonwireless.com/support/3-way-calling-faqs/ retrieved 3/10/16.
[15] Cf. ProgrammerWorld.Net: What are advantages and disadvantages of VoIP? URL: http://faq.programmerworld.net/voip/voip-advantages-disadvantages.htm retrieved 3/10/16.

owing to the circumstance that VoIP basically involves the data transfer between two IP addresses. Furthermore, the subjection of the VoIP call to the quality of the Internet connection results in the downside that in case of a parallel use of the computer the quality most likely will deteriorate if not become absolutely inaudible. At last the phone connection via the Internet exposes private data to the Internet, which presents a general risk due to the risk of malware, viruses, identity theft, phishing attacks or call tampering.[16]

3 Instant messaging tools

3.1 Slack and Skype – a brief introduction

A very common, high-rated and free instant messaging application for Windows is Skype, which was founded in 2003. It is used by more than 300 million people worldwide. Further, is has been taken over by Microsoft for $8.5 billion in the year 2011. The amount of minutes used by Skype video calls add up to amazing 2 trillion.[17]

On the other hand, there is the fast-growing instant messaging application Slack showing up with about 600.000 users and an active user's growth rate located between 3-5 % each week. It was launched in the beginning of 2014. Its users collectively spend more than 100 million hours on Slack.[18] Even though there is a free version for small teams or unlimited evaluation, commercial versions of Slack are available called Standard, Plus and Enterprise.[19]

3.2 SWOT-Analysis by the comparison of Skype and Slack

The following SWOT-Analysis is supposed to compare Skype and Slack as representative tools for free and commercial instant messaging tools, respectively.

Strengths: Skype presents a very versatile instant messaging tool with additional features. It is free and very easy to download for every user and available for both

---

[16] Cf. ISP Reviews: Advantages & Disadvantages of VoIP. URL: http://www.isp-reviews.org/voip_benefits_disadvantages.htm retrieved 3/10/16.
[17] Cf. Digital Stacks / Gadgets: By the Numbers: 24 Amazing Skype Statistics and Facts. URL: http://expandedramblings.com/index.php/skype-statistics/ retrieved 3/10/16.
[18] Cf. ibid.
[19] Cf. #slack: Pricing Guide. URL: https://slack.com/pricing retrieved 3/10/16.

smartphones be it for Android or iOS as well as tablets.[20] While offering a possibility to chat, the user can also send files via Skype by a user-friendly drag and drop function.[21] Moreover, VoIP calls can be made by clicking on contact names, dialing on the pad by means of the softphone interface while received, missed and whole recent conversations via VoIP and instant messaging are saved in a history. At the same time the receiver can look into the caller's profile, accept, receive or block calls at wish. Further, one can look for contacts, send the respective ones a request to be added to their contact list. Besides conference calls can be held via Skype including video calls within instant messaging chats or separately. Additionally, voicemails can be recorded and voice messages can be sent to contacts without the necessity to call them. Also, the user can choose between private conversations with another person or a talk in a group that the person himself or another member of the contact list has created. At last the user can create a profile involving a picture and some private information.[22] Own observations have revealed that one can choose between a single and compact sidebar view besides the option to split the Skype window. For the purpose of questions concerning Skype, the user is connected to a very clearly and simply structured website with large and legible texts. Also, the menu of the messenger is not overloaded with buttons but pretty user-friendly. Concerning social media, Skype only integrates with Facebook as individuals can log in with their Facebook account.

Slack, on the other hand, has an onscreen helping guide called Slackbot, which makes you become familiar with the main features of the application such as sending and reading messages, opening a profile and inviting people. The helping bot also comes handy when it comes to reminding the user of a date since Slackbot alerts you by a sound call. Like Skype it offers a clean or a more efficient compact view while its window appears spacious and attractive and the font is legible. Uploading files can be carried out very conveniently by clicking the "+" symbol left to the text bar at the bottom. At the same time Slack offers a range of dealing with sending files as one can monitor the accessibility concerning special members of groups or individuals in general.

---

[20] Cf. Online Sciences: What are the advantages and disadvantages of Skype? URL:
http://www.online-sciences.com/technology/what-are-the-advantages-and-disadvantages-of-skype/
retrieved 03/11/16.
[21] Cf. Small Business Chron: Advantages of Skype. URL: http://smallbusiness.chron.com/advantages-skype-63207.html retrieved 03/11/16.
[22] Cf. About Tech: Skype – Major Features. URL:
http://voip.about.com/od/voipsoftware/a/skypefeatures.htm retrieved 03/11/16.

Additional special features that Slack provides are a spellcheck function, the option to delete messages and files manually. Various actions such as transferring and locating files, instant messaging as well as asking Slackbot a question can be handled in the same window. Furthermore, Slack integrates the common services such as GoogleDrive, Dropbox and Twitter. All commercial subscriptions involve free applications for PC, Mac, Android and iOS.[23]

Weaknesses: A major weakness of Skype is obviously its dependency on the Internet connection when it comes to functions such as VoIP and video conferences. Regarding phone calls, a Wi-Fi or 3G service is required besides the fact that international VoIP calls cost money. In addition, it shows deficits in its degree of security since it has been publicly known that hackers have wiretapped top officials via Skype. Further, the quality of voice and sound is not satisfactory. In addition, there are lots of camera failures.[24] Besides the troubleshooting options are pretty limited as there is no hotline for customer service but only the option of online requests. If a customer wants to use a landline phone together with Skype, the options are very restricted for Skype is only compatible to a few brands and types of landline phones.[25] In contrast to Slack, Skype does not integrate any other common software that is able to send you messages. Skype is also known for showing an incorrect online/offline status of a member on the contact list. Visually, features such as coloring and sounds are relatively limited. Also, messaging extras such as typing bold or italic or alternative texting features are not available on Skype.[26]

As opposed to Skype, Slack is offered in a free version only with limitations. Also, Slack itself does not offer audio or video calls itself but needs to connect to Skype or Google Hangouts for this. Using Slack in a company, it can only connect the user to other members of the business. A further major weak spot is the defective notification system as it neither alerts the user of the number of missed messages nor of unread messages

---

[23] Cf. Blackwell, L. (2013): Meet slack, a chat tool with collaboration talent to spare. URL: http://www.pcworld.com/article/2079103/meet-slack-a-chat-tool-with-collaboration-talent-to-spare.html retrieved 03/11/16.
[24] Cf. Online Sciences: What are the advantages and disadvantages of Skype? URL: http://www.online-sciences.com/technology/what-are-the-advantages-and-disadvantages-of-skype/ retrieved 03/11/16.
[25] Cf. Schieltz, M. (eHow): Disadvantages of using Skype. URL: http://www.ehow.com/list_5939079_advantages-skype.html retrieved 03/11/16.
[26] Cf. Biz 3.0 Time Doctor: Slack vs. Skype: Which Team Chat Did We Choose? URL: http://biz30.timedoctor.com/slack-versus-skype-team-chat-app/ retrieved 03/11/16.

in each conversation. Along with this goes the insufficiency that the user is not revealed if messages were received while the computer was offline. Associated with this, Slack cannot be utilized if the user is offline. At last it has been reported by a number of users that Slack would affect their computer performance.[27]

Opportunities: First and foremost, Skype provides the essential opportunity of communicating to other individuals or groups via instant messaging or VoIP calls, which simultaneously enables audio and video conferences. This can be very advantageous for both private purposes and smaller groups to keep in touch and businesses to hold meetings or conferences as well, in particular if long distances need to be bridged. This goes hand in hand with very low or any costs for calls and messaging expanding the possibility of using Skype for everyone with an Internet connection. People can join conversations from different locations and therefore save money and time to take care of private or professional affairs. The download version for Android and iOS broadens the user group and increases the accessibility at the same time. VoIP calls can be established to other computers involving Skype or other regular phones worldwide.[28] Because it does not require high system resources, even PCs with lower performance can make use of Skype as a communication tool. Further, Skype's notification mechanisms ensure that the user gets notified of the quantity and quality of messages, in particular businesses can benefit from that knowing that they have already taken care of a business affair.[29]

Providing the Slackbot, an all-round helping assistant, the user quickly gets to know how to deal with Slack and is able to take care of his business more rapidly. This is backed by the convenience of the "+" button right next to the text bar facilitating and accelerating the mailing of files, which in particular offices within enterprises can benefit from concerning frictionless workflows during a fast-paced economically globalized age. Also, private or business appointments can't be forgotten anymore due to the reliable Slackbot alert. From a more visual perspective, the appealing design and pragmatic layout of the window makes Slack also interesting for user's who appreciate

---

[27] Cf. ibid.
[28] Cf. Online Sciences: What are the advantages and disadvantages of Skype? URL:
http://www.online-sciences.com/technology/what-are-the-advantages-and-disadvantages-of-skype/
retrieved 03/11/16.
[29] Cf. Biz 3.0 Time Doctor: Slack vs. Skype: Which Team Chat Did We Choose? URL:
http://biz30.timedoctor.com/slack-versus-skype-team-chat-app/ retrieved 03/11/16.

optical features. At the same time compared to Skype, Slack offers manifold possibilities concerning the ability to share for example private data with selected individuals or recipient groups. Extra features such as a spellcheck function reduce the likelihood of sending spelling errors, which might be essential when the sender intends to leave a good impression in order to make a future deal or applying for a job. As a result, Slack encourages multitasking besides a commodious accessibility to mainstream online platforms such as Dropbox and GoogleDrive, which enable the user the upload and download of large amounts of files. Potential misunderstandings or stressful processes of compromise settlement regularly present considerable challenges concerning communication and interaction in the framework of a department team within a corporation. Regarding this, Slack provides simplifications by allowing taking care of various actions simultaneously.[30]

Threats: When it comes to urgent video calls, Skype is apparently in advance of Slack as the latter software needs to connect to the former one to make video calls feasible. Simultaneously, Skype exhibits a higher degree of inconvenience concerning the range of sort and search options, which can waste valuable time and energy of a company personnel. On the other hand, unread messages of great importance are entirely ignored by Slack, which can result into severe consequences if for example deadlines or further significant messages are communicated while the computer is switched off. As it is no rarity that some employees of an enterprise stay longer than others, left messages cannot reach the recipient on the following working day making it necessary to make an additional effort writing the note down on paper or saving it on a word processing program. As regard to notifications which represent an essential component of instant messaging tools, Slack demonstrates multiple malfunctions adding to the already mentioned lack of accessibility of the recipient. Furthermore, the high requirement in system resources in the case of Slack, may cause computers with resources on the lower edge of the spectrum to freeze unpredictably, hence leaving formerly running processes or files unsaved and provoking loss of time and expenses. From a financial perspective, Slack might be a secondary option for the average user since the full version of Skype is always available for free while the free version of Slack is limited in its usage. Additionally, in particular situations such as flights, certain rural areas or in well insulated buildings, the internet connection via smartphone might

---

[30] Cf. ibid.

just not be sufficient enough, which in these contexts consequently disqualifies using Slack in contrast to Skype.[31]

3.3 Result

In sum, even if Slack excels in providing a much more manageable and visually convenient communication platform within a community, more advanced and capable search functions as well as a higher tolerability with other software, the SWOT-analysis comes to the resolution that Skype presents the more multi-facetted and therefore more effective instant messaging tool on various levels, in particular given by the possibility to make low-cost VoIP calls, its comprehensive notification system including its recording of missed messages during time the hardware has been shut down, very clearly structured instructions steps and its compatibility with lower system resources. Since it is expected that both the smaller community for private purposes and the multi-billion enterprise wish for the additional feature of VoIP calls, this critical factor that Slack can only meet this demand with the help of a subsequent connection to Skype or Hangouts, has a substantial impact on the verdict. At the same time Skype's dependency on an Internet connection cannot be ignored although it is compensated by numerous possibilities and locations individuals can connect their respective hardware to the World Wide Web as well as the recording of missed messages and calls while being offline.

4   Conclusion

Having evaluated benefits, weaknesses, opportunities as well as threats of online communication tools involving e-mail, VoIP telephony and two common instant messaging tools, it can be concluded that e-mail represents a medium that will continue to exist in the world of online communication due to their ability to transmit information rapidly and their enabling attaching files at the same time but will certainly not be found among the top communication means of the future.

---

[31] Cf. ibid.

Concerning communicating via voice, VoIP presents a great and cost-efficient potential to be extended, in particular different sizes of enterprises worldwide. In order to gain a higher level of popularity and application, technical advances are inevitable such as an improvement of the voice quality and a higher degree of protection from harming viruses and malware coming from the Internet. In case of having optimized technical deficits, VoIP telephony will very likely be in the frontline of the next generation technology, in particular indicated by the fact that they have already been included in worldwide leading instant messaging tools such as Skype.

By the example of Skype and Slack, instant messaging tools have proven their functional capability and development capacity in retrospect. The combination of both tools results in wide-ranging communication options and extras such as all-time availability for third parties, VoIP-calls, the convenient transmission of data, a commodious visual work surface and a more effective way of multitasking benefitting organizations particularly. Therefore, advanced instant messaging tools with additional functions together with the facilitation of prompter and more organized communicative exchange as well as a more user-friendly working surface will play a more and more decisive role in the context of online communication tools.

Bibliography

#slack: Pricing Guide. URL: https://slack.com/pricing retrieved 3/10/16.

About Tech: Skype – Major Features. URL:
http://voip.about.com/od/voipsoftware/a/skypefeatures.htm retrieved 03/11/16.

Alexander, P. (Entrepreneur, publ.): Should your business use instant messaging?
URL: http://www.entrepreneur.com/article/81050 retrieved 03/10/16.

Biz 3.0 Time Doctor: Slack vs. Skype: Which Team Chat Did We Choose? URL:
http://biz30.timedoctor.com/slack-versus-skype-team-chat-app/ retrieved 03/11/16.

Blackwell, L. (2013): Meet slack, a chat tool with collaboration talent to spare. URL:
http://www.pcworld.com/article/2079103/meet-slack-a-chat-tool-with-collaboration-talent-to-spare.html retrieved 03/11/16.

Davey, T. et al. (2004): Instant messaging. Functions of a new communication tool.
Indiana: University of Notre Dame, Department of Anthropology, Blum, S. (publ.).

DeSantis, M. (2008): Understanding Voice over Internet Protocol. US-CERT (publ.)
URL: https://www.us-cert.gov/sites/default/files/publications/understanding_voip.pdf
p.3., retrieved 3/10/16.

Digital Stacks / Gadgets: By the Numbers: 24 Amazing Skype Statistics and Facts.
URL: http://expandedramblings.com/index.php/skype-statistics/ retrieved 3/10/16.

Federal Communications Commission: Voice Over Internet Protocol (VoIP). URL:
https://www.fcc.gov/general/voice-over-Internet-protocol-voip retrieved 3/10/16.

Hertlein, K. M.; Ancheta, K.: Advantages and Disadvantages of Technology in
Relationships: Findings from an Open-Ended Survey. In: The Qualitative Report
2014, vol. 19, article 22.

ISP Reviews: Advantages & Disadvantages of VoIP. URL: http://www.isp-reviews.org/voip_benefits_disadvantages.htm retrieved 3/10/16.

Kumar, A.: An overview of Voice Over Internet Protocol (VoIP). In: Rivier College
Online Academic Journal, vol. 2, no. 1, spring 2006.

Online Sciences: What are the advantages and disadvantages of Skype? URL: http://www.online-sciences.com/technology/what-are-the-advantages-and-disadvantages-of-skype/ retrieved 03/11/16.

ProgrammerWorld.Net: What are advantages and disadvantages of VoIP? URL: http://faq.programmerworld.net/voip/voip-advantages-disadvantages.htm retrieved 3/10/16.

Schieltz, M. (eHow): Disadvantages of using Skype. URL: http://www.ehow.com/list_5939079_advantages-skype.html retrieved 03/11/16.

Small Business Chron: Advantages of Skype. URL: http://smallbusiness.chron.com/advantages-skype-63207.html retrieved 03/11/16.

TechandSeo: Advantages and Disadvantages of VoIP. URL: http://www.techandseo.com/2015/11/advantages-and-disadvantages-of-voip-voice-over-Internet-protocol retrieved 3/10/16.

To, N. M. L. (2008): Influence of emoticons on message interpretation in computer mediated communication. Academia.

Verizon wireless: Support. 3-Way Calling FAQs. URL: http://www.verizonwireless.com/support/3-way-calling-faqs/ retrieved 3/10/16.

Wikispaces: The Internet as a Communication tool. URL: https://techforinstructionandassessment.wikispaces.com/The+Internet+as+a+Communication+Tool retrieved: 03/06/16.

www.ingramcontent.com/pod-product-compliance
Lightning Source LLC
La Vergne TN
LVHW042321060326
832902LV00010B/1656